Football in America

THE PRO FOOTBALL HALL OF FAME

DiscoverRoo
An Imprint of Pop!
popbooksonline.com

Robert Cooper

abdobooks.com

Published by Pop!, a division of ABDO, PO Box 398166, Minneapolis, Minnesota 55439.

Printed in the United States of America, North Mankato, Minnesota.

052019
092019

THIS BOOK CONTAINS RECYCLED MATERIALS

Cover Photo: Gene J. Puskar/AP Images
Interior Photos: Gene J. Puskar/AP Images, 1, 11, 26–27, 30; mpi34/MediaPunch /IPX/AP Images, 5; Ben Liebenberg/AP Images, 6, 8–9; Bob Rossiter/The Canton Repository/AP Images, 7; NFL Photos/AP Images, 12–13, 31; AP Images, 14–15, 16 (bottom); iStockphoto, 15, 21; Pro Football Hall of Fame/AP Images, 16 (top); David Durochik/AP Images, 17 (top); Tony Tomsic/AP Images, 17 (bottom), 20; Paul Abell/Invision for NFL/AP Images, 19, 22; Ron Schwane/AP Images, 23; Scott Boehm/AP Images, 25; Tony Dejak/AP Images, 28; Steve Helber/AP Images, 29

Editor: Nick Rebman
Series Designer: Jake Nordby

Library of Congress Control Number: 2018964851

Publisher's Cataloging-in-Publication Data

Names: Cooper, Robert, author.

Title: The Pro Football Hall of Fame / by Robert Cooper.

Description: Minneapolis, Minnesota : Pop!, 2020 | Series: Football in America | Includes online resources and index.

Identifiers: ISBN 9781532163791 (lib. bdg.) | ISBN 9781644940525 (pbk.) | ISBN 9781532165238 (ebook)

Subjects: LCSH: Football--Juvenile literature. | American football--Juvenile literature. | National Football League--Juvenile literature. | Pro Football Hall of Fame (U.S.)--Juvenile literature.

Classification: DDC 796.33264--dc23

WELCOME TO DiscoverRoo!

Pop open this book and you'll find QR codes loaded with information, so you can learn even more!

Scan this code* and others like it while you read, or visit the website below to make this book pop!

popbooksonline.com/pro-football-hall-of-fame

*Scanning QR codes requires a web-enabled smart device with a QR code reader app and a camera.

TABLE OF

CONTENTS

CHAPTER 1

CALL TO THE HALL

Brian Urlacher is ready for his big moment. The former football player steps onto the stage. For 13 years, he was a linebacker for the Chicago Bears. But now it's time for one of the greatest

WATCH A VIDEO HERE!

Brian Urlacher makes a speech after becoming a member of the Hall of Fame.

moments of his entire career. He will become a member of the Pro Football Hall of Fame.

DID YOU KNOW?

Brian Urlacher was one of eight people voted into the Hall of Fame in 2018.

THE GOLD JACKET

Each Hall of Fame player receives a gold jacket. This jacket is available only to members of the Hall of Fame. The player wears his jacket when he is inducted. He also wears the jacket at other events related to the Hall of Fame.

Every year, hundreds of players compete in the National Football League (NFL). But only the very best are **inducted** into the Hall of Fame. Becoming a member is a huge honor.

A bust of Brian Dawkins is on display at the Hall of Fame.

Philadelphia Eagles star Brian Dawkins receives his gold jacket in 2018.

Every summer, a **ceremony** welcomes new members into the Hall of Fame. It takes place in Canton, Ohio.

Fans pack the stadium in Canton to watch the Hall of Fame ceremony.

Thousands of fans travel to watch. The event is a time to celebrate the NFL's best players.

CHAPTER 2

A PROUD HISTORY

The Pro Football Hall of Fame opened in 1963. It is in Canton, Ohio. That may seem like a strange location. After all, Canton does not have an NFL team. But that was not always the case.

LEARN MORE HERE!

The Hall of Fame has a dome shaped like a football.

The NFL was created in Canton. In 1920, several teams met there to form a league. One of them was the Canton

The Canton Bulldogs compete in an early NFL game in the 1920s.

Bulldogs. Canton had one of the first great pro football teams. The Bulldogs won two NFL titles in the 1920s.

Chicago Bears fullback Bronko Nagurski was one of the first 17 players to be inducted.

The Hall of Fame **inducted** its first class in 1963. Seventeen players entered the Hall that year. Today, the Hall includes more than 300 members.

DID YOU KNOW?

Four players from the Canton Bulldogs are members of the Hall of Fame.

TIMELINE

1920
The NFL is founded in Canton, Ohio.

1962
Workers begin building the Hall of Fame in Canton.

1963
The first players are inducted into the Hall of Fame.

1967
Emlen Tunnell becomes the first black player to join the Hall of Fame.

1995
The Hall of Fame museum is expanded to include a movie theater.

2014
Ray Guy becomes the first punter to be inducted.

CHAPTER 3

MAKING THE CUT

Each year, **sportswriters** choose the new Hall of Fame members. The writers meet a few days before the Super Bowl. They have to pick at least four people. But they cannot pick more than eight.

LEARN MORE HERE!

Hall of Famer Brett Favre (left) greets Packers quarterback Aaron Rodgers at an award show before the Super Bowl in February 2019.

Pittsburgh Steelers head coach Chuck Noll (right) entered the Hall of Fame in 1993.

A player cannot enter the Hall of Fame right away. He has to wait five years after he **retires**. This rule does not apply to coaches. They can be **inducted** as soon as they retire.

TEAMS WITH THE MOST HALL OF FAMERS

NFL greats Ed Reed, Champ Bailey, and Gil Brandt appear onstage after being announced as Hall of Famers in February 2019.

The new members are announced the day before the Super Bowl. After that, it's time for the players to plan for their big day. They start thinking about what they will say during their speeches.

The Chicago Bears and Baltimore Ravens compete in the 2018 preseason game in Canton.

DID YOU KNOW?

Every year, a **preseason** game takes place in Canton. It happens the same weekend as the Hall of Fame **ceremony**.

CHAPTER 4

THE HALL OF FAME EXPERIENCE

The Hall of Fame is more than a place that honors NFL greats. It's also a place where fans can learn about the history of pro football. They can visit the Hall of Fame museum.

COMPLETE AN ACTIVITY HERE!

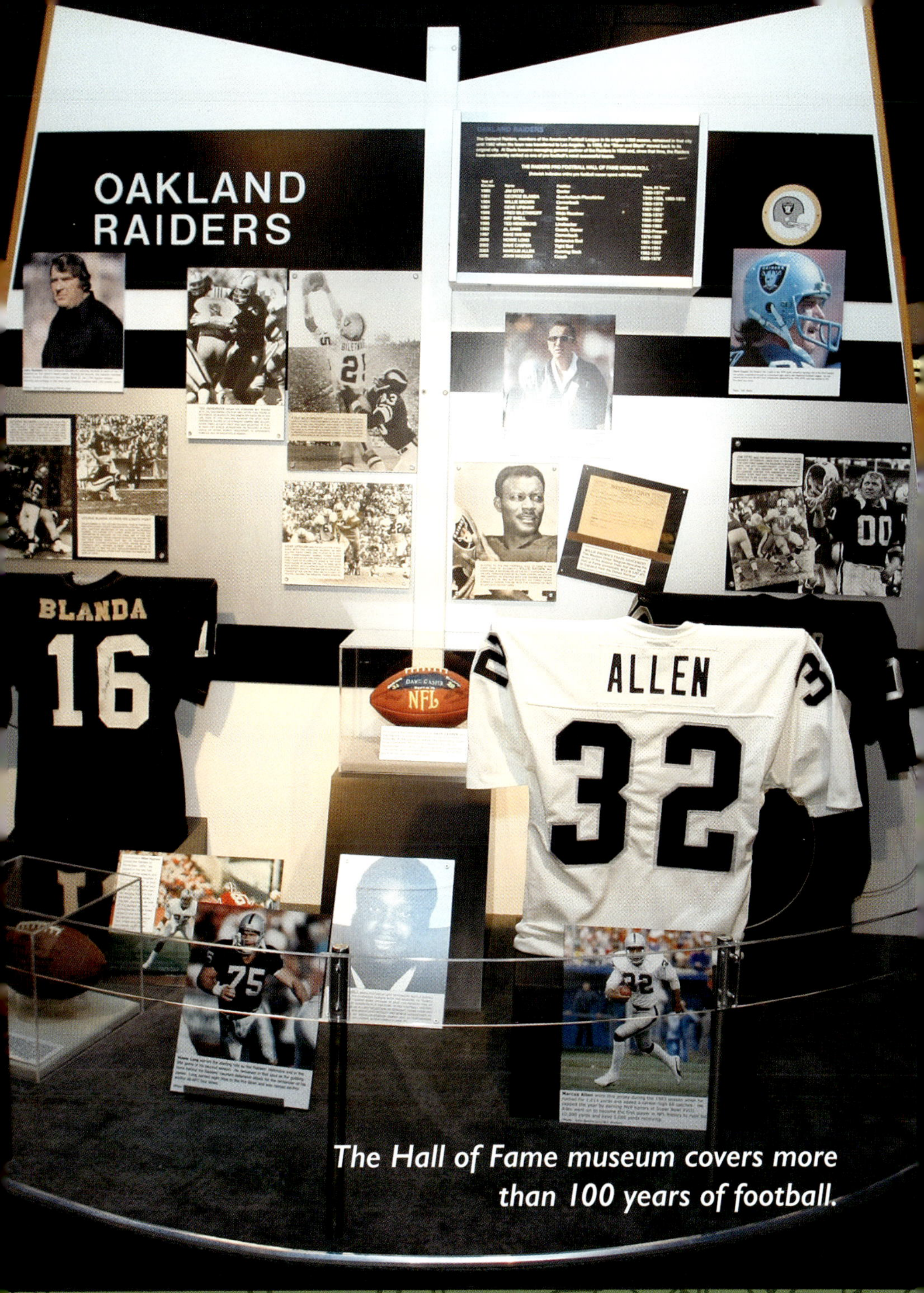

The Hall of Fame museum covers more than 100 years of football.

One part of the museum shows all the players who have been **inducted**. Each player has a **bust**. There is also a

Players stand with their busts after being inducted into the Hall of Fame.

summary of his career. The museum is a great place for fans to learn about the players and teams.

A visitor checks out jerseys, balls, and other items in a Hall of Fame exhibit.

Fans can see balls from famous games. They can also see **interactive** exhibits. Fans can use touch screens to view photos or videos. They can even play video games.

DID YOU KNOW?

When a team wins the Super Bowl, each player on the team gets a ring. The Hall of Fame museum has a ring from every Super Bowl.

Each Super Bowl ring has a different design.

MAKING CONNECTIONS

TEXT-TO-SELF

Would you ever want to visit the Pro Football Hall of Fame? Why or why not?

TEXT-TO-TEXT

Have you read books about another sport that has a hall of fame? What makes the Pro Football Hall of Fame unique?

TEXT-TO-WORLD

The Pro Football Hall of Fame honors great athletes. How else do people honor the ones they respect or admire?

GLOSSARY

bust – a sculpture of a person's head.

ceremony – an event that celebrates an important occasion.

induct – to let someone into a club or organization.

interactive – allowing the user to get involved in what is going on.

preseason – a set of games that happen before the regular season.

retire – to stop working, usually because of old age.

sportswriter – someone who writes about sports for a newspaper or website.

INDEX

ONLINE RESOURCES

popbooksonline.com

Scan this code* and others like it while you read, or visit the website below to make this book pop!

popbooksonline.com/pro-football-hall-of-fame

*Scanning QR codes requires a web-enabled smart device with a QR code reader app and a camera.